26 BIG Things Small Hands Do

By Coleen Paratore

Illustrated by Mike Reed

free spirit
PUBLISHING®

Helping kids
help themselves
since 1983

To teach a child the alphabet is an honor indeed. When my three sons were younger, we had such fun learning those 26 letters that would one day open the magical doors to reading and writing. They proudly called out, "A, B, C," as their small hands gripped pencils to carefully copy each shape.

One winter morning, my then 4-year-old son Connor and I were driving to the library when it began to snow. I could see him beaming in the rearview mirror.

"Look, Connor," I said. "*Sssss*-snow. What letter does snow start with?"

The smile left Connor's face. He looked serious, or was it annoyed?

After a while, he said, "You don't *spell* snow, Mom. You *enjoy* it."

I share this memory because it reminds me that while we adults have so much to teach our children, they have much to teach us as well.

26 Big Things Small Hands Do is a celebration of just some of the ways in which children make our world a better place. As you read aloud, you can encourage children to think about what their hands do and to mimic the positive actions throughout, starting with their small hands applauding *you* and ending with your big hands applauding *them*.

What a gift it is to know and love a child. I am reminded of this each time I see a poem called "The Hand" hanging on my office wall. My son Connor wrote it when he was 7, and around the words are his small handprints. The poem begins, "With this hand I can play ball," and ends, "With this hand I can pick up snow."

My son had learned to "spell snow" and was still enjoying it, too.

Coleen Paratore

Your hands are small,
but they do BIG
things that make this
a wonderful world.

Aa

Small hands **a**pplaud.

Small hands **build.**

Bb

Cc Small hands **c**olor rainbows
red, yellow, blue.

And small hands **draw**, too.

Dd

Ee Small hands **e**xplore the earth for treasures.

Small hands feed.   Ff

Gg

Small hands **give** gifts made with love.

Small hands **help**. Hh

Ii

Small hands invite
new friends to play,

and small
hands join.

Jj

Kk

Small hands **k**indle kindness.

Small hands lend.

Ll

Mm

Small hands **make** music in marching bands.

Small hands nestle. **Nn**

Oo

Small hands open books
and travel far.

Small hands **p**lant.

Pp

Qq

Small hands **q**uestion so everyone learns.

Small hands **r**ecycle.

Rr

Ss Small hands **s**ign love without a sound,

and small hands **t**each.

Uu

Small hands **u**ncover beautiful things.

Small hands **v**olunteer.

Vv

Ww

Small hands water so gardens will grow.

Small hands **x** and o.

Xx

Yy

Small hands . . . YES! Hurray! High five!

And small hands
ZZZZ**ZZ**ZZ**Z**zzz
Goodnight.

Zz

From **A-B-C** to **X-Y-Z**,
such BIG things
small hands do.
You make our world
a better place . . .

Now big hands
clap for *you*.

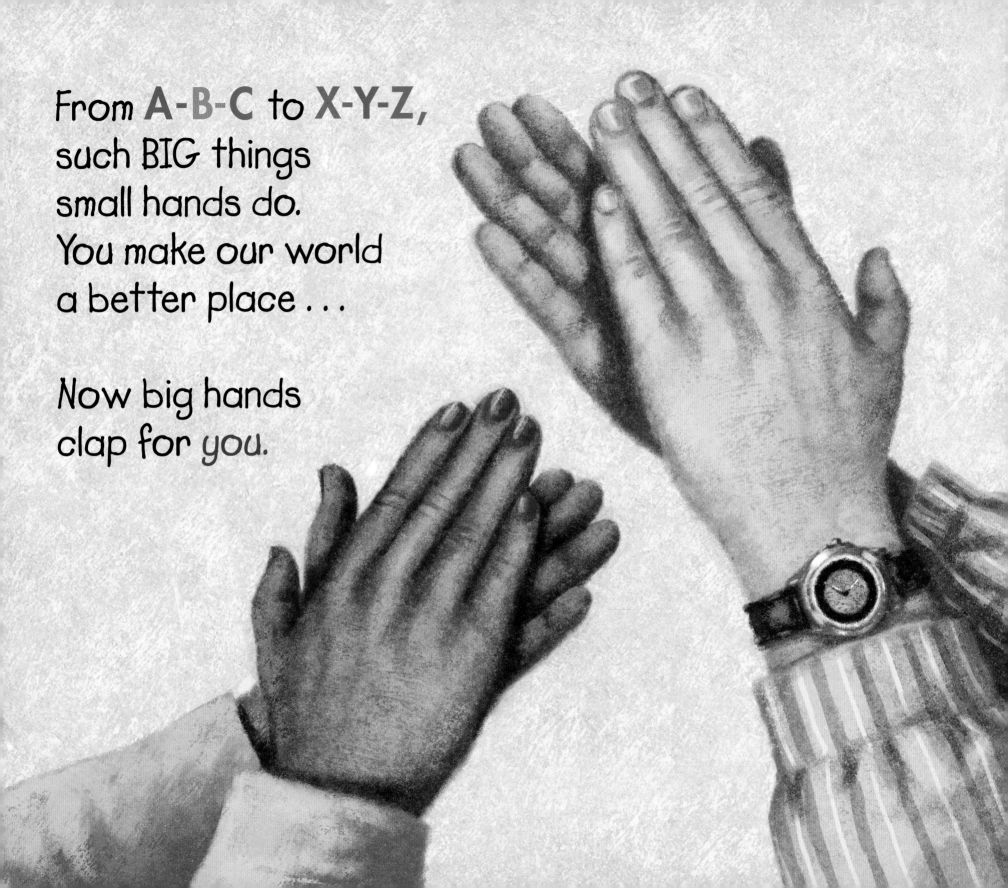

With love to my three sons—Christopher, Connor, and Dylan—
who taught me the "big things"when they were small;
and with special thanks to Connor, who inspired this book.—C.P.

For Isabel, from Uncle Mike.—M.R.

Library of Congress Cataloging-in-Publication Data
Paratore, Coleen, 1958–
   26 big things small hands do / by Coleen Paratore ; illustrated by Mike Reed.
      p. cm.
   ISBN-13: 978-1-57542-306-7
   ISBN-10: 1-57542-306-5
   1. Hand—Social aspects. 2. Hand—Physiology. 3. Alphabet. I. Reed, Mike, 1951–, ill. II. Title. III. Title: Twenty-six big things small hands do.
   GT498.H34P37 2008
   612.97—dc22

                                                                          2008007490

Edited by Elizabeth Verdick
Design by Marieka Heinlen

10 9 8 7 6 5 4 3 2 1
Printed in Hong Kong

Free Spirit Publishing Inc.
217 Fifth Avenue North, Suite 200 • Minneapolis, MN 55401-1299
(612) 338-2068 • help4kids@freespirit.com • www.freespirit.com